The Wild West

Through Time

Published in 2009 by The Rosen Publishing Group, Inc.
29 East 21st Street, New York, NY 10010

Created and produced by Nicholas Harris and Claire Aston,
Orpheus Books Ltd

U.S. editor: Kara Murray
Illustrator: Mark Stacey
Consultant: Christina Parker

Library of Congress Cataloging-in-Publication Data

Aston, Claire.
The Wild West through time / Claire Aston.
p. cm. — (Fast forward)
Includes index.
ISBN 978-1-4358-2799-8 (library binding)
1. West (U.S.)—History—Juvenile literature. 2. West (U.S.)—Social
conditions—Juvenile literature. 3. West (U.S.)—Social life and
customs—Juvenile literature. 4. Frontier and pioneer life—West
(U.S.)—Juvenile literature. I. Title.
F591.A88 2009
978—dc22
2008031801

Printed and bound in China

FAST FORWARD

The Wild West
Through Time

illustrated by Mark Stacey

text by Claire Aston

PowerKiDS
press.

New York

Contents

Introduction

Imagine you are in the western United States hundreds of years ago. It is a vast, empty land, with nothing but grassy plains and herds of grazing buffalo. It may not seem very likely, but there is an exciting story to tell about what will happen here later. The events take many years to unfold, but you can follow them in this book.

The story is like a journey. It is not a journey you can make by plane, car or ship. In fact, you don't have to go anywhere at all. You are about to travel through time. With each turn of the page, the date moves forward a few years. You are still in the same place, but notice how many things change from one date to the next. Each date—each stop on your journey—is like a new chapter.

The time when the Indians had the land to themselves, the arrival of new settlers from overseas, the building of farms, villages and towns, the coming of the railroad, the days of cowboys, outlaws and gunfights all tell the story of what has become known as the Wild West.

Use the thumb index to travel through time! This will help you make a quick comparison between one scene and another, even though they show events that took place some years apart. A little black arrow on the page points to the date of the scene illustrated on that page.

The Year AD 600

American Indians have lived on the Great Plains for thousands of years. They travel around on foot, hunting the herds of buffalo that roam the plains. Buffalo provide the Indians with most of their food. The buffalos' skins, fur and bones are useful for making clothes, tepees (tents), weapons and tools.

As soon as the lookouts spot a herd of buffalo, the hunters begin to stalk them. Carefully herding the animals along valleys, they slowly drive them toward a strong wooden enclosure, called a corral, that they have already built.

As the buffalo approach the corral, the hunters run toward them, shouting, waving skins and sticking them with flint-tipped spears to make the buffalo run into the corral. The hunters need great skill and courage to herd the huge animals without being stomped on or gored by their sharp horns.

THE AMERICAN INDIANS

People first settled in North America between 35,000 and 15,000 years ago (the date is uncertain). During the Ice Age, the sea level was lower than it is today. It was possible to walk from northeastern Siberia to Alaska. Hunters followed their prey—mammoth, deer and other animals—into this new land. Over the years, people spread out to all parts of the Americas. Where game was plentiful, in forests and on the Great Plains, people continued to live by hunting. In some places, they turned to farming.

AD 600

1800

A few years later

The 1840s

A few years later

The 1860s

A few years later

In a few more years

The 1870s

A few years later

Early 1900s

Today

The Year 1800

The lives of the Plains Indians have changed a great deal since the arrival of European settlers. The Spaniards brought horses, which quickly became prized possessions among the Indians. Horses allow them to travel great distances at high speed and to hunt buffalo with greater success. A man on horseback can now gallop alongside a running buffalo, using his spear or bow and arrow to kill the buffalo. Hunting on horseback also makes herding buffalo into corrals or driving them over cliffs easier for the hunters.

8

The Indians trade, steal and breed horses. This has led to fighting among tribes. Instead of working together to find food, parties of Indians now attack one another's camps. Some tribes have become famous for their swift and fierce attacks.

An attacking party sweeps into the camp of a neighboring tribe on horseback, taking everyone by surprise. They drive away horses and steal stored meat and grain. As well as spears and bows and arrows, the attackers now have guns.

Neighboring tribes often have fierce battles. Warriors gain honor from a brave and victorious fight.

AD 600

1800

A few years later

The 1840s

A few years later

The 1860s

A few years later

In a few more years

The 1870s

A few years later

Early 1900s

Today

9

A Few Years Later...

A group of Indians from the Sioux tribe have set up camp close to where their lookouts have sighted a herd of buffalo. While the hunters ready their horses and weapons for a day's hunting, the women prepare buffalo hides that they will make into clothing, tepees or bags. They stretch and pin the hides out to dry, cleaning them with sharp bone scrapers. Other women hang fresh buffalo meat

Tepee

Drying meat

Learning archery

Baby carried in cradleboard

Cleaning hides

onto a wooden rack to dry. This will be the main food supply for the group when the buffalo have moved on.

The children of the camp run around and play, but there is also work to be done. Girls help their mothers, while boys learn how to use weapons.

Inside a tepee, one of the older members of the group tells stories to the children, to teach them about the tribe's history. The tepee has warm hides on the floor and wooden backrests.

ois

Chief

Backrest

1800

A few years later

The 1840s

A few years later

The 1860s

A few years later

In a few more years

The 1870s

A few years later

Early 1900s

Today

11

Travelers often carved their names into rocks at landmarks along their journey. They also wrote notes on buffalo skulls and left them along the trail, to encourage or warn later travelers.

The 1840s

A group of white settlers from far away in the East are traveling across the plains in search of new farming land in the West. The settlers travel in wagons drawn by mules, horses or oxen. As evening falls, the settlers draw their

Looking at maps

Buffalo chips

Repairing a wagon wheel

wagons into a circle to keep out wild animals.

The men repair their wagons, feed the animals and consult maps. The children play while women prepare dinner over a fire of buffalo chips. They depend on the food they carry, as food is scarce on the plains.

Indians

Wagon

AD 600

1800

A few years later

The 1840s

A few years later

The 1860s

A few years later

In a few more years

The 1870s

A few years later

Early 1900s

Today

Most of the gold hunters panned for gold in streambeds. They swirled water and mud around in a metal pan, trying to find flakes or nuggets of gold.

A Few Years Later...

A group of families from the East are traveling westward toward Oregon and California. They have been inspired by reports from previous travelers, who tell of rich farmland and a pleasant climate. On their journey west, however, the group have met other travelers who have given up and turned back. They warn the families to expect hunger, thirst, heat and cold. Deadly illnesses such as cholera are common and have killed many people.

The group hope they will have more luck. One of their fears, however, is attack by fierce Indian tribes. But the Indians they meet are friendly and looking to trade goods, although some request money for passing through their

Trading blankets

Buffalo hides

Trading guns

lands. The Indians are used to white settlers. They have traded with fur trappers and adventurers, known as mountain men, for many years.

As the wagon train pauses to rest, the Indians trade buffalo hides and dried buffalo meat for blankets, guns and luxuries such as beads and mirrors. The Indians also help the travelers plan the next part of their route.

THE GOLD RUSH

Not all travelers along the Oregon and California trails were in search of rich farmland. The Mormons, a Christian group, left the East where they were hated and attacked for their beliefs. They settled on the deserted shores of the Great Salt Lake.

In 1848 gold was discovered in California. Tens of thousands of men went there in the hope of making a fortune to take home to the East, but few actually did. Towns grew up around mining areas. Although many were quickly deserted when the gold ran out, some became large cities.

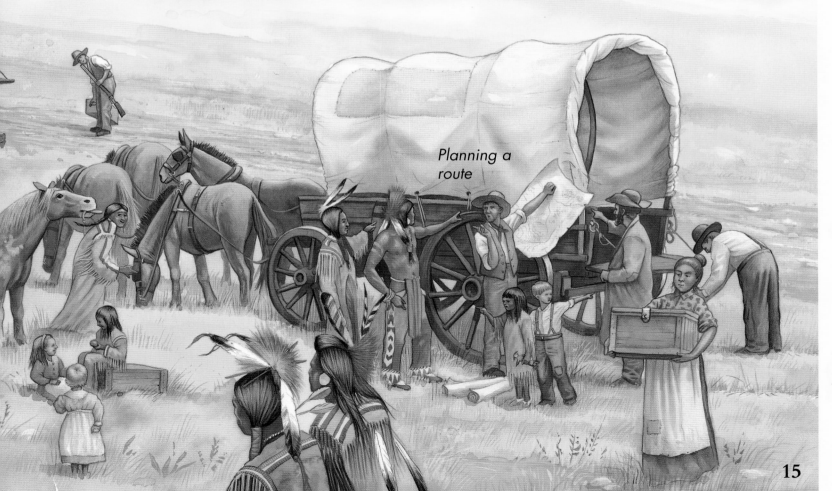

Planning a route

AD 600

1800

A few years later

The 1840s

A few years later

The 1860s

A few years later

In a few more years

The 1870s

A few years later

Early 1900s

Today

Life on the plains was much harder than the homesteaders had expected. There were floods and snow in the winter and droughts, fires and storms in summer. Worst of all were the insects. Thick swarms of grasshoppers could suddenly settle on a homestead and eat all the crops in a matter of hours. The homesteaders were left with nothing.

The 1860s

Settlers are now setting up homes on the Great Plains. They come not only from the eastern states but also from abroad. This family has come from Eastern Europe. They have almost finished building their farm, or homestead.

With little wood to be found on the plains, their house is built from sod, slabs cut from the ground. The heavy ground is baked hard by the sun and hard to cut, so the family must wait until it has been softened by rain. Special heavy plows are needed to prepare the ground for sowing crops.

Collecting buffalo dung

Cutting sods

The women take care of the family and cook the meals. They collect dried buffalo or cow dung to fuel the fires and antlers, which will later be ground down into fertilizer for the crops. The nearest homestead is miles (km) away, so visitors are always welcome.

LAND FOR FREE

To encourage more people to settle on the plains, the U.S. government passed the Homestead Act of 1862. This set aside large areas of land and gave people a plot of 160 acres (65 ha) free as long as they built a house and lived there for five years. Many settlers took up this opportunity in a hurry.

Among the new settlers were black people who had once been slaves but were now free. They were now able to build their own homes and farms.

Grass fire

Sod house

Buffalo dung

Antlers

Plowing

AD 600

1800

A few years later

The 1840s

A few years later

The 1860s

A few years later

In a few more years

The 1870s

A few years later

Early 1900s

Today

17

A Few Years Later...

The homestead is under attack from a group of Indians. They are angry that their homelands are being taken over by white settlers. The Indians fear for the safety of their people and way of life and have decided to fight back.

Some of the men of the homestead are inside the house with the women and children, shooting through the windows. Other men take cover outside, trying to shoot the Indians as they gallop past. The Indians drive away cattle and start fires around the house. They are armed with guns as well as bows and arrows.

The cavalry of the U.S. army protected settlers in the vast areas of land between the eastern United States and the new West. Cavalry soldiers were based at camps along the westward trails. People often settled near a camp for protection from Indians.

Cavalry

Suddenly a warning shout goes up from one of the Indians and a cheer comes from the homesteaders. A group of armed U.S. cavalry soldiers from a nearby camp are arriving to rescue the homesteaders. The Indians take a few last shots and gallop away at top speed.

ON THE WARPATH

When people began to settle in the West, the U.S. government promised the Indians that the Great Plains would always belong to them. However, as more people moved west, more land was needed. The government moved the Indians into smaller territories and finally into reservations, areas of land occupied by one tribe but run by white traders and settlers. This began years of terrible wars, in which many people from both sides were killed.

Shooting through window

Homesteaders

Firing burning arrow

AD 600

1800

A few years later

The 1840s

A few years later

The 1860s

A few years later

In a few more years

The 1870s

A few years later

Early 1900s

Today

19

The first ranchers settled on the Texas prairies. They used cowboys to herd their cattle north across the Great Plains to the railroads, to be carried to markets in the East. Later ranchers set up homes on the Great Plains, closer to the railroads.

Early ranches were unfenced and cattle could wander for miles (km). Barbed wire fencing meant that ranchers could keep their own cattle on their land and wild cattle out.

On the bare, dry plains, many farms and towns used windmills to pump water up from under the ground. In railroad towns these were especially important to provide water for the steam trains.

Route of new railroad

Windmill

Tents

Wagon

Church

TAILORS SHOP

PUBLIC SCHOOL

Stagecoach

Photographer

In a Few More Years...

The area where the homestead used to stand has now grown into a small town. A new railroad is being built, which will pass by the town carrying goods and cattle. People have come here to set up homes and businesses.

Many of the buildings in the small town are only shacks or tents, homes to the men who are working to build the railroad. There are also wooden buildings, such as a church and a bar. A small school has been built for the children of the few families living in the town.

As the railroad workers haul the rails into place, other men are building barbed wire fences to make cattle pens. Telegraph poles are being erected next to the railroad, so that messages can be passed from one end of the country to the other. A stagecoach is being loaded with passengers' baggage and mail. Until the railroad is completed, the stagecoach is the fastest way to travel.

Building fences

Telegraph pole

Supervisor

Building railroad tracks

21

AD 600

1800

A few years later

The 1840s

A few years later

The 1860s

A few years later

In a few more years

The 1870s

A few years later

Early 1900s

Today

The 1870s

The small town has grown rapidly since the railroad was completed. Wood has been brought in by rail to build more houses, as well as shops and hotels. There are wooden walkways outside the buildings on the main streets. In front of the walkways are wooden hitching rails for people to tie up their horses.

Busy cattle towns often drew criminals known as outlaws to them. Cattle rustlers tried to steal cattle as cowboys drove them toward the town. Other outlaws were robbers, highwaymen and even murderers. Some outlaws, such as Billy the Kid and Jesse James, became very well known. People wrote stories about their adventures, and myths grew up about how they lived and died.

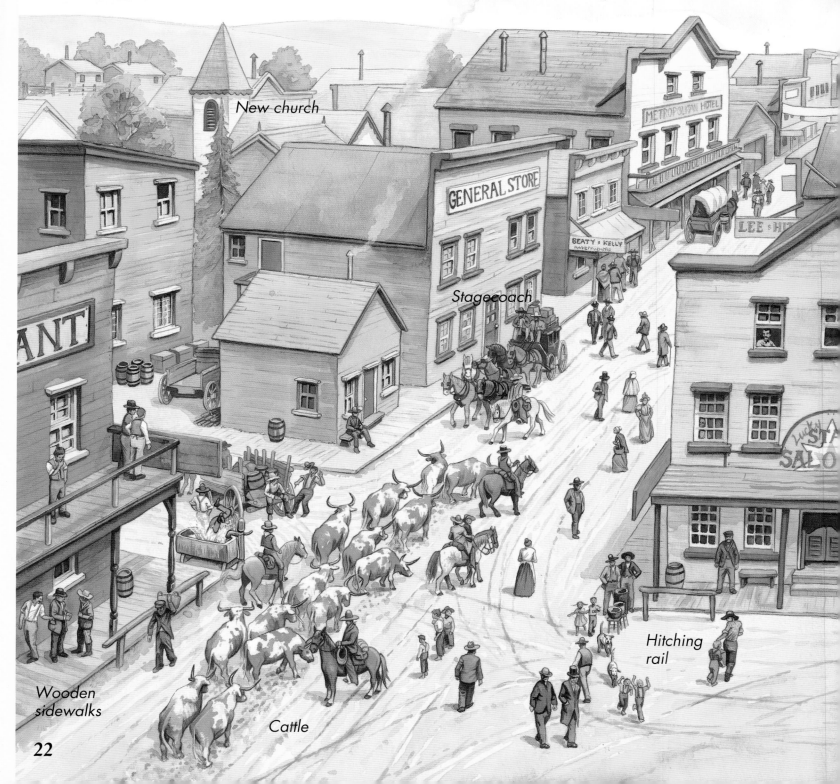

New church

GENERAL STORE

BEATY & KELLY

METROPOLITAN HOTEL

LEE & HIT

Stagecoach

Lucky STA SALO

Wooden sidewalks

Cattle

Hitching rail

The town plays an important part in the cattle trade business. Cowboys drive cattle from ranches in the South across the plains to the town. They herd the cattle into pens and then load them onto trains headed for markets in the East.

When the cattle are loaded, the cowboys can enjoy life in town. There are plenty of boarding houses to stay in, and saloons, bars and dance halls for them to relax in after weeks or even months on the cattle trails.

Old church

Telegraph wires

Herding cattle onto train

Cattle pens

Steam train

ELITE LODGINGS

Stables

LIVERY

Cowboys

23

AD 600

1800

A few years later

The 1840s

A few years later

The 1860s

A few years later

In a few more years

The 1870s

A few years later

Early 1900s

Today

A Few Years Later...

The town is even bigger and has become very rowdy. Outlaws come into town to steal horses and to rob people. The cowboys that swarm the town also cause a lot of trouble. They spend most of the money they have earned from the cattle drive on drinking and betting, which often causes arguments and fighting.

There were several kinds of law officers. Town marshals *(above)* made sure that their town was law-abiding and dealt with small crimes such as fights. Sheriffs were in charge of counties. Both sheriffs and marshals had deputies to help them and also used groups, or posses, of local people when hunting an outlaw. U.S. marshals and their deputies took charge of a territory or state. They dealt with those accused of more serious crimes and brought them to court to face a judge.

Saloon and boarding house

STORE

Jail

Grocery store

Marshal

Posse

In the saloon, a drunken fight has started because someone has cheated in a card game. In the street outside, passersby run for cover as a gunfight breaks out. The town marshal hurries out of the jail to break up the fight before too many people get hurt.

LAW AND ORDER

At first, no one took charge of law and order in the new towns that grew up across the West. Instead local people, called vigilantes, grouped together to catch outlaws and hang them for their crimes. However, the vigilantes also attacked people who were not criminals and their own personal enemies.

As the towns grew larger, the U.S. government sent in marshals, sheriffs and judges. These lawmen often helped clean up a town, but some were criminals themselves.

Hotel and saloon

Stables

Gunfight

AD 600

1800

A few years later

The 1840s

A few years later

The 1860s

A few years later

In a few more years

The 1870s

A few years later

Early 1900s

Today

25

Early 1900s

It is a time of progress and excitement. The town has grown into a busy city, its main street lined with shops, electric street lights and paved sidewalks. Telephone wires tie businesses and homes together. People wander into the large department stores to buy new inventions such as vacuum cleaners and electric irons. Many visit the cinema, or nickelodeon, to see a cowboy movie.

After years of battles in which the Indians suffered most, the Indian Wars between the U.S. army and the tribes reached their height at the Battle of Little Bighorn in 1876. General George Custer's forces were crushed by the Indians. The Indians had been forced onto reservations where they had to obey U.S. law, even if they had not taken part in the wars. In 1890, stories of the Ghost Dance, which would make the settlers disappear excited the Indians. The army panicked, leading to the killing of 153 Sioux Indians at the Massacre at Wounded Knee. This was the last battle—the Indians were conquered.

Nickelodeon

Trolley car

Hot-dog seller

Trolley tracks

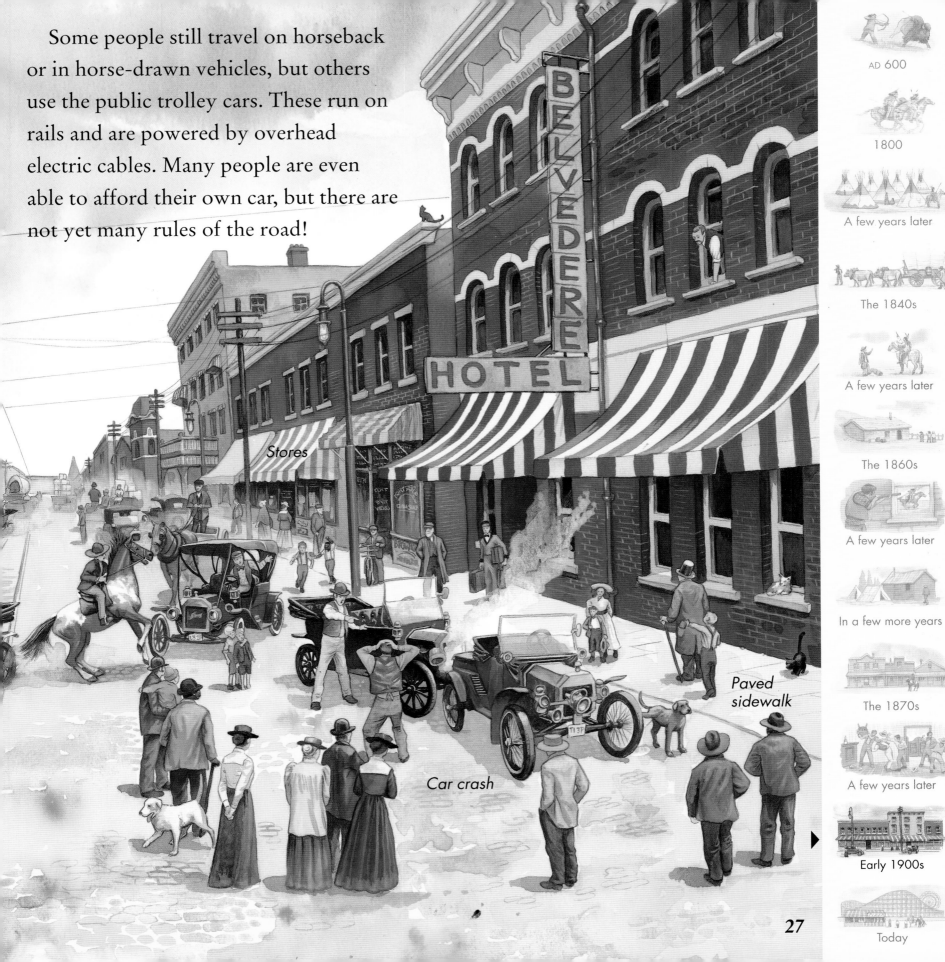

Some people still travel on horseback or in horse-drawn vehicles, but others use the public trolley cars. These run on rails and are powered by overhead electric cables. Many people are even able to afford their own car, but there are not yet many rules of the road!

Stores

Paved sidewalk

Car crash

BELVEDERE

HOTEL

AD 600

1800

A few years later

The 1840s

A few years later

The 1860s

A few years later

In a few more years

The 1870s

A few years later

Early 1900s

Today

Wild West shows have been performed since the late 1800s, when Buffalo Bill Cody toured America and Europe with a show called Buffalo Bill's Wild West Show. The entertainment included shooting displays, stagecoach holdups, rodeo riding and battles with Indians. The shows spread a false image of Indians as fierce, ruthless attackers of harmless settlers.

The Wild West has always been a popular subject for moviemakers. Stories about bands of daring outlaws and the lawmen who hunt them down often lead to an exciting gunfight at the end of the movie.

Today

On the outskirts of the modern city, with its towering skyscrapers and fast pace of life, a Wild West theme park has been built. It has thrilling rides, such as roller coasters, and many shows. People dressed as cowboys ride up and down the streets. A crowd gathers to watch a show in which a shoot-out takes place. The actors make this seem funny and exciting.

Mock hanging

Cavalry parade

Stagecoach

Cowboy skills

Pony rides

A rodeo show exhibits real-life cowboy skills, such as bull roping and riding. Children can go for rides on a pony, in a stagecoach or even on a miniature railway. There are many fast-food restaurants and a saloon with music and dancing girls. Visitors come from miles (km) around to experience a little of the Wild West, but how closely does this match what real life in the Wild West was like?

Skyscrapers

Roller coaster

Miniature railway

Shootout show

AD 600

1800

A few years later

The 1840s

A few years later

The 1860s

A few years later

In a few more years

The 1870s

A few years later

Early 1900s

Today

29 ▶

Glossary

cattle trail (KA-tul TRAYL) The route taken by cowboys driving herds of cattle. There were several main cattle trails, including the trail north from Texas to towns on the railroad.

cavalry (KA-vul-ree) A group of soldiers that fought on horseback.

corral (kor-AL) A pen for cattle or buffalo herded together for killing. A protective circle of wagons made by white settlers was also called a corral.

deputy (DEH-pyuh-tee) Second in command to a marshal or sheriff.

Great Plains (GRAYT PLAYNZ) A vast tract of land in North America lying between the Mississippi River to the east and the Rocky Mountains to the west. Before white people settled there, the plains were barren grasslands grazed by buffalo and occupied by a number of different Indian tribes.

homestead (HOHM-sted) A farm established by settlers on the Great Plains. Encouraged by the offer of cheap land from the U.S. government, homesteaders first moved onto the plains in the 1860s.

marshal (MAR-shul) A U.S. marshal was appointed by the U.S. government. He was responsible for bringing to justice people accused of serious crimes,

like robbing a train. A town marshal dealt with smaller matters such as fights and brawls.

nickelodeon (nih-keh-LOH-dee-un) An early cinema or movie theater. The entrance charge was five cents, or one nickel.

outlaw (OWT-law) Someone who led a life of crime, often robbing banks and trains for money and valuables.

posse (PAH-see) A group of men called out by a town marshal or sheriff to hunt down an outlaw.

ranch (RANCH) A large farm on the Great Plains where people known as ranchers raised cattle.

reservations (reh-zer-VAY-shunz) Areas where Indian tribes were forced to live by the U.S. government. They were made to give up their way of life.

rodeo (ROH-dee-oh) A roundup of cattle or an exhibition of cowboy skills.

sheriff (SHER-if) A law officer appointed by a county. He was like a local policeman.

stagecoach (STAYJ-kohch) A carriage, usually pulled by six horses, that carried passengers and mail across the West. It made regular stops, known as stages, on the way.

telegraph (TEH-lih-graf) The sending of messages by electrical signals along wires.

tepee (sometimes spelled "tipi") (TEE-pee) A large cone-shaped tent made of buffalo hides hung on poles. Most Plains Indians lived in villages made up of tepees.

travois (truh-VOY) A horse-drawn sled used by the Indians to haul their tepees and belongings.

vigilantes (vih-jih-LAN-teez) A group of people who took charge of law and order for themselves.

Index

Web Sites

Due to the changing nature of Internet links, PowerKids Press has developed an online list of Web sites related to the subject of this book. This site is updated regularly. Please use this link to access the list: www.powerkidslinks.com/fastfor/wildwest/